A VISION OF INDIA

BOOK 1

THE COUNTRY

Written by

Swarn Khandpur

Illustrated by

Pradeep Sathe

navNeet

NAVNEET PUBLICATIONS
(INDIA) LIMITED

F 531

© 1997 Navneet Publications (India) Ltd.

Published by Navneet Publications (India) Ltd.
Bhavani Shankar Road, Dadar, Mumbai – 400 028. INDIA
Tel. 430 7286   Fax : 437 2568

Offices :
Navneet House, Gurukul Road, Memnagar,
Ahmadabad – 380 052.   Tel. 745 3995 / 745 3010
Sita Park, 18, Shivaji Nagar, Near Bharat English School,
Pune – 411 005.   Tel. 326364
Agge Apartments, Agyaramdevi – S.T. Stand Road,
Nagpur – 440 018.   Tel. 724411
30, Sriram Nagar, North Street, Alwarpet,
Chennai – 600 018.   Tel. 453614
6 – 1 – 142, 1st floor, Padmarao Nagar,
Secunderabad – 500 025.   Tel. 761 2354

Cover design by : D.Y. Acharekar

Edited by : Chandralekha Maitra

The Publishers gratefully acknowledge the help extended to this
project by the Khandpur Resource Library.

Printed at : Printmann, Mumbai – 400 013

INDIA ISBN 81-243-0356-8

Price : Rs. 50.00

CONTENTS

INTRODUCTION

There has been a long-felt need for attractive and informative books about modern day India. Books that are neither textbooks nor encyclopaedias, but are specifically attuned to the visual and reader-friendly requirements of the contemporary child.

A VISION OF INDIA has been conceived as a continuing series, planned with the purpose of unveiling India's modern profile for young readers. The individual volumes will then be compiled into a unique compendium on India. The information has been presented in the form of wide-ranging questions and answers, supported by colourful and accurate illustrations. The textual style has been kept simple but incorporates a wealth of interesting and varied knowledge.

This first book, **A VISION OF INDIA** Book 1 – THE COUNTRY, acquaints the reader with India as a country, its physical setting and political framework, its variety of people, their languages and scripts, national symbols and holidays, as well as other related information.

This series, dealing with post-independence India and the national identity, is perceived as a valuable addition to schools and libraries, as well as to the bookshelf of every child who is proud to be a citizen of India.

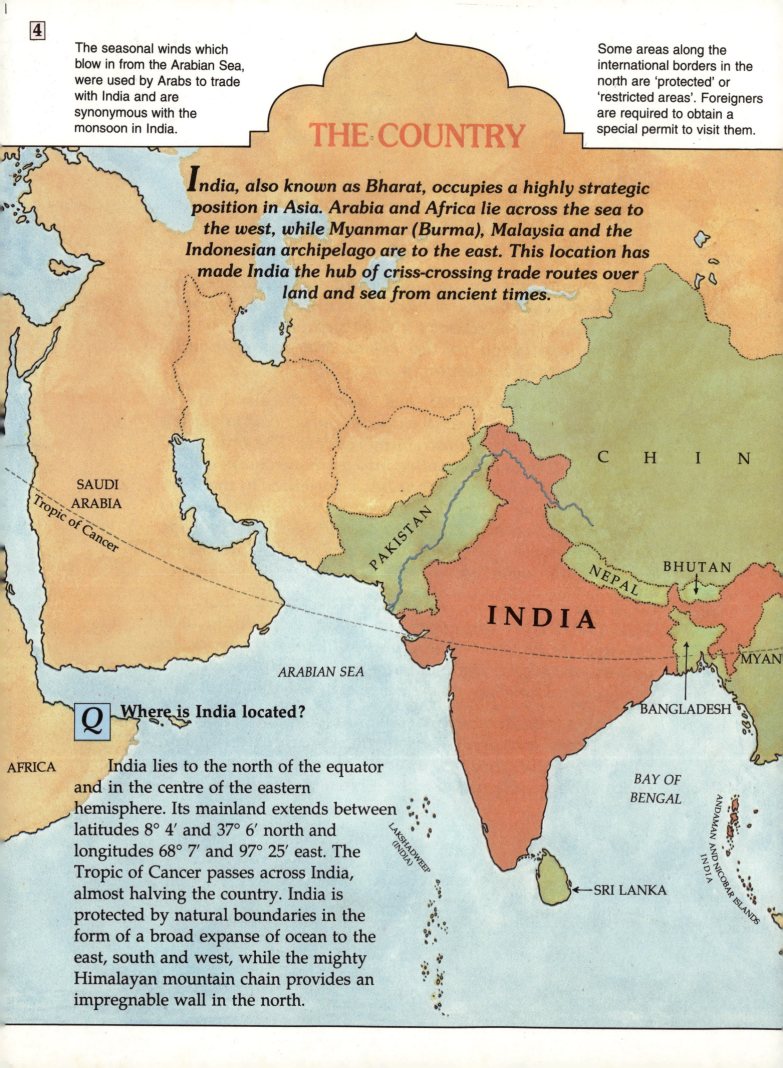

The seasonal winds which blow in from the Arabian Sea, were used by Arabs to trade with India and are synonymous with the monsoon in India.

Some areas along the international borders in the north are 'protected' or 'restricted areas'. Foreigners are required to obtain a special permit to visit them.

THE COUNTRY

India, also known as Bharat, occupies a highly strategic position in Asia. Arabia and Africa lie across the sea to the west, while Myanmar (Burma), Malaysia and the Indonesian archipelago are to the east. This location has made India the hub of criss-crossing trade routes over land and sea from ancient times.

Q **Where is India located?**

India lies to the north of the equator and in the centre of the eastern hemisphere. Its mainland extends between latitudes 8° 4′ and 37° 6′ north and longitudes 68° 7′ and 97° 25′ east. The Tropic of Cancer passes across India, almost halving the country. India is protected by natural boundaries in the form of a broad expanse of ocean to the east, south and west, while the mighty Himalayan mountain chain provides an impregnable wall in the north.

*Bharata, the fearless son of King Dushyanta and Shakuntala, could count the teeth of a lion's cub while playing with it. India was named **Bharat** after this valiant ruler of ancient India.*

India's border with Pakistan is shared by four of her states—Jammu and Kashmir, Punjab, Gujarat and Rajasthan.

Q How did India get her name?

India derived its name from the river Indus, which the early Aryans called the Sindhu (ocean), meaning a huge sheet of water. This great river, in ancient times, formed the western boundary of India. The Persians, who conquered the country around the river Sindhu, pronounced the letter 'S' as 'H', thus terming the region beyond the Sindhu as 'Hindu' or 'Hind'.

With the coming of the Muslims, the name became *Hindustan* and the people inhabiting the land were known as *Hindus*. Europeans, however, called India the country of the Indus.

Q How big is India?

India, it is often said, is not a country but a sub-continent. This is because India is as large as the whole of the sub-continent of Europe, excluding Russia.

Extending over 3,000 kilometres from north to south and nearly 3,000 kilometres from east to west, India covers a land area of over 32,00,000 square kilometres, which is 2.4 per cent of the earth's surface. The Andaman and Nicobar Islands, in the Bay of Bengal and Lakshadweep, in the Arabian Sea, are integral parts of the territory of India. It ranks as the seventh largest country in the world and after China, the second largest in Asia.

Q Who are India's neighbours?

India shares its political borders with Pakistan in the west and Bangladesh and Myanmar (Burma) in the east. Its northern boundary touches China, Nepal and Bhutan. The Gulf of Mannar and the Palk Strait separate India from Sri Lanka.

Q How big is the Bay of Bengal?

Although the Hudson Bay in Canada is regarded as the largest bay in the world, the Bay of Bengal has, in fact, a greater area. Its shoreline, however, is shorter than that of the Hudson Bay.

	Bay of Bengal	Hudson Bay
Area	→ 21,72,000 sq.kms.	8,22,300 sq.kms.
Shoreline	→ 3,621 kms.	12,268 kms.

THE PHYSICAL SETTING

India has a land frontier of 15,200 kilometres and a coastline of over 6,000 kilometres. She has the towering mountain ranges of the Himalayas in the north. South of them lie the Great Plains or the Indo-Gangetic plain, formed by the mighty rivers of northern India. The Thar desert is located to the west, while the Deccan Plateau of peninsular India, is in the south, with fertile coastal strips on either side. The country thus enfolds a panorama of physical contrasts.

THE HIMALAYAS

 How extensive are the Himalayas?

The Himalayas (meaning Abode of Snow), are the highest mountains in the world. They stand like a gigantic wall all along India's northern frontier. They extend from the borders of Myanmar in the east to the western limits of Kashmir, covering a distance of 2,500 kilometres. They are also the world's youngest mountain system.

The Himalayas consist of three parallel mountain ranges – the Great Himalayas (Himadri), the Lesser Himalayas (Himachal) and the foothills (Shiwaliks). The Great Himalayas contain 9 of the 14 highest peaks in the world, Mount Everest (in Nepal) being the highest.

 Which is the highest mountain peak in India?

K2 is the highest mountain peak in India. It is the second highest peak in the world and is alternatively known as Mount Godwin-Austen. As it lies in the north of Kashmir, in the Karakoram range, it is still known worldwide by its original survey number K (Karakoram) 2. It is 8611 metres high, only 237 metres less than Mount Everest.

 When did an all-Indian expedition first conquer Mt. Everest?

The first two Indian expeditions to Mt. Everest, undertaken in the years 1960 and 1962, were beaten back by hostile weather conditions. The third expedition, in 1965, under M.S. Kohli, created a record by putting nine climbers on top of the mountain.

 Where is the Nanga Parbat?

The Nanga Parbat, which literally means Naked Mountain, marks the western end of the Great Himalayan range. This 8126-metre-high peak, is the third highest mountain in India.

 What are duns?

The duns are broad, flat valleys found between the Himachal and Shiwalik ranges of the Himalayas. The town of Dehra Dun is located in one such dun.

☐ Mountaineering, as a sport, began about 100 years ago. Several attempts were made to conquer Mount Everest. However, the first to reach its summit were Edmund Hillary and Tenzing Norgay, on May 29, 1953.

☐ Bachendri Pal was the first Indian woman to set foot on the highest point on earth at 1:07 pm, on May 23, 1984.

☐ The 8598-metre-high, Kanchenjunga, the second highest peak of the Himalayas in India, can be viewed from Darjeeling, in West Bengal. Conquered by the Indian Army expedition of 1977, led by Col. Narendra Kumar, Kanchenjunga presents a much more difficult climbing challenge than Mt. Everest.

☐ The only cold desert in India is Ladakh, surrounded by the snow-covered Karakoram range of the Himalayas. Situated at a height of 4878 metres, Ladakh is also the highest plateau in the country.

☐ Although Mount Everest is the world's highest mountain, Mauna Kea in Hawaii is taller! This is because Mauna Kea has its base in the seabed and when measured from base to top, it is higher than Everest by 1355 metres.

☐ Mount Kailash, in the central Himalayas, is said to be the abode of Lord Shiva. In painting and sculpture, the Lord is shown in deep meditation, seated on a tiger skin and surrounded by snowy peaks.

There are more than 100 mountain peaks over 7000 metres high in Asia, mainly in the Himalayas. Sikkim has the largest number of such peaks.

The highest mountain peak in each of the continents is:

● Asia	Everest	8,848 M
● South America	Aconcagua	6,960 M
● North America	McKinley	6,194 M
● Africa	Kilimanjaro	5,895 M
● Europe	Elbrus	5,633 M
● Antarctica	Vinson Massif	5,140 M
● Australasia	Mt. Wilhelm	4,509 M

 What is Purvachal?

The eastern ranges of the Himalayas are referred to as Purvachal, because of their location in the east (Purva). They are neither so high nor so widespread as the western ranges, but have very dense forests. The Patkai Bum and related ranges such as the Naga Hills, Garo Hills and the Lushai Hills, run along India's border with Bangladesh and Myanmar.

 What are mountain passes?

The Himalayas, the highest mountain system in the world, are normally impassable. However, the ranges in the northwest contain some gaps which provide natural routes across them. These gaps, called 'passes', have long served as trade routes while also enabling invaders to intrude into India. The most well-known of the passes is the Khyber Pass.

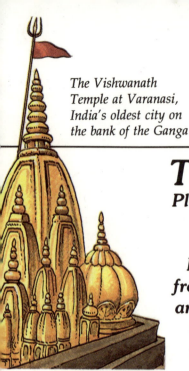

The Vishwanath Temple at Varanasi, India's oldest city on the bank of the Ganga

THE GREAT PLAINS

The Great Plains of India, also known as the North Indian Plains or the Indo-Gangetic Plain, lie at the foothills of the Himalayas. They have been built up by the great river systems dominated by the Indus, the Ganga, the Brahmaputra and their tributaries. These plains extend from the Punjab in the west to Assam in the east, covering an area of 652,000 square kilometres. Here were founded the major kingdoms of the past, the earliest centres of Aryan civilization and the most ancient cities of India.

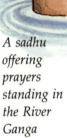

A sadhu offering prayers standing in the River Ganga

Q How were the Great Plains formed?

Millions of years ago, the area which is now called the Great Plains, was a vast stretch of water. It formed the bed of a great sea, which geologists call the Tethys Sea. The southern shore of this sea was the ancient Deccan plateau and to its north lay the landmass of central Asia. Geological changes caused the southern mass to push against the northern mass and out of the sea arose a huge mountain range – the Himalayas. While they were in the process of elevation, they left a deep depression. This depression gradually filled up with gravel, sand and silt, called alluvium, brought down by the Himalayan rivers. This level stretch of fertile land then came to be known as the Great Plains.

Tsangpo

NEPAL

BHUTAN

Brahmaputra

Yamuna

Ganga

INDIA

BANGLA DESH

The Great Plains, being alluvial, is one of the world's most extensive and fertile areas and is, therefore, very densely populated.

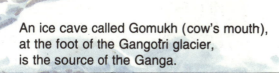

An ice cave called Gomukh (cow's mouth), at the foot of the Gangotri glacier, is the source of the Ganga.

Ganga – The Sacred Mother

 Q **Why is the Ganga called the Bhagirathi?**

It is believed that the Ganga descended to earth from heaven in answer to the prayers of the mythical king, Bhagirath, in order to redeem the condemned souls of his ancestors. Thus, at its source, lying in the Himalayas in Uttar Pradesh, the river is known as the Bhagirathi. After flowing for about 175 kilometres, the Bhagirathi is joined by the rivers Alaknanda and Mandakini, at Deva Prayag. The combined waters then take on the name Ganga.

Q **How big is the Gangetic plain?**

The Ganga is the longest river in India. During the course of its journey of 2507 kilometres, from its source to the sea, at the Bay of Bengal, it is joined by several tributaries – the Yamuna and Son from the right and the Gomti, Ghaghara, Gandak and Kosi from the left. Its basin, therefore, forms the largest part of the Great Plains and covers almost one-fourth of the total land area of the country.

Q **Which two rivers form the world's largest delta?**

The Ganga divides itself into two streams near Bengal – one flowing as the Hooghly into West Bengal and the other, as the Padma, into Bangladesh. About 480 kilometres from the Bay of Bengal, the Padma is joined by the mighty Brahmaputra and together they form the world's largest delta, in the Indo-Bangladesh region.

The Indus – Sindhu

 Q **Which tributary of the Indus is believed to flow underground?**

The Sarasvati, celebrated both as a river and a deity in the hymns of the *Vedas*, was an important tributary of the Indus. Once broad and big, the Sarasvati is now lost in the sands of the Thar desert. Interestingly, it is believed that flowing underground, the Sarasvati joins the Ganga at her confluence with the Yamuna at Prayag in Allahabad. The place where the three rivers meet is known as Triveni Sangam and is venerated as very holy.

☐ The Sarasvat Brahmins, inhabiting areas around the Sarasvati River in the Punjab, take their name from the river.

Ganga, on her mount the crocodile

Yamuna, on her mount the tortoise

Alexander the Great is said to have built 12 pillars to the Greek gods on the banks of the Beas before turning back to Macedonia.

The traditional deity of the Sindhis is Udero Lal, a god associated with the river Indus.

Q **Which are the five famous tributaries of the Indus?**

The Indus or River Sindhu, while journeying from Tibet to the Arabian Sea, meets five great rivers – Ravi, Beas, Satluj, Jhelum and Chenab. Before the partition of India in 1947, the land of these rivers was called Punjab (five waters). After partition, although only the Satluj and Beas rivers flow through the Punjabi region in India, yet the Indian state in that region is still called Punjab.

Mount Kailash

Mansarovar Lake

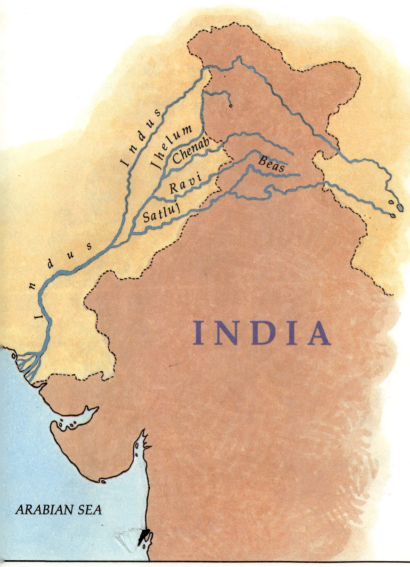

INDIA

ARABIAN SEA

Q **Where is the source of the River Indus?**

The Indus rises in the Mount Kailash range about 100 kilometres north of the Manasarovar Lake. It flows northwest in Tibet before entering Jammu and Kashmir. Meeting a number of rivers on the way, it cuts through, at one place, a gorge 5,200 metres deep. The Indus then enters Pakistan and joins the Arabian Sea near Karachi.

The Brahmaputra, the only river in India with a male name, is known as Tsang-Po, in Tibet; Jamuna, in Bangladesh; and Padma, after its confluence with the Ganga and Meghna, when it meets the waters of the Bay of Bengal.

The *duars* in Assam (the marshy area at the foothills of mountains), is the home of the famous one-horned rhinoceros.

Brahmaputra– Lord Brahma's Son

 Where is the island of Majuli situated?

The island of Majuli is on the river Brahmaputra in Assam. It was once the largest freshwater island in the world. Due to severe erosion and floods in the river, the island has been eroded and reduced to one third of its original size in less than two decades.

 With which river does the Brahmaputra share the largest delta in the world?

The Brahmaputra, from its source near the Mansarovar Lake to the mouth of the Bay of Bengal, is one of the world's longest rivers. It is even longer than the Ganga, by 400 kilometres. After flowing 2704 kilometres through northeastern India and Bangladesh, it joins the Ganga to form the largest delta in the world.

Q Why is the Brahmaputra called the 'Red River' of India?

The Brahmaputra has more than 40 major tributaries in Assam. During the monsoon, this giant river swells and spills over its banks, causing devastating floods. These waters, after mingling with the red soil of Assam, take on a reddish hue, making it the 'Red River' of India.

The Brahmaputra river in flood

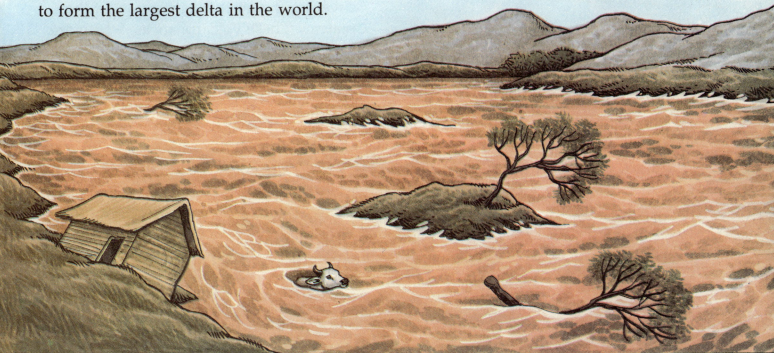

One of the Buddhist caves at Ajanta, hollowed out of a cliff of the Deccan plateau

The Aravali Hills, in the north-western corner of the Deccan plateau, are some of the oldest mountains in the world.

THE DECCAN PLATEAU

 Which is the oldest plateau in India?

The Deccan plateau is the oldest tableland of the south Indian peninsula. It was once a part of a gigantic landmass that connected India with Africa. Owing to repeated geological pressures, this part broke off from the main mass and exists, to this day, as one of the remaining blocks of that ancient land. It stands 300 to 900 metres above sea level.

 How did the plateau acquire the name Deccan?

The name Deccan or *Dakhin*, is from the Sanskrit word *dakshin*, which means 'the south'. The plateau lies south of the Vindhya range (1050 kilometres long), which separates it from the alluvial Indo-Gangetic plain. The plateau is shaped like a triangle, bounded on the east and west by mountain ranges known as the Eastern and Western Ghats. The two Ghats meet to form the southern tip of the triangle.

 How does the west coast of India differ from the east coast?

The coastal strip between the Western Ghats and the Arabian Sea is narrow, while that between the Eastern Ghats and the Bay of Bengal is broad. Moreover, the rivers on the west coast are short and swift and do not end in deltas. On the east coast, a number of rivers form deltas. There are more ports and natural harbours in the west than in the east.

 What is the Deccan Trap?

It is a step-like rock formation covering the north-western part of the plateau. These volcanic rocks, which are several hundred metres thick and made of Basalt, were formed about 70 million years ago. The word 'trap' comes from the Swedish term for steps.

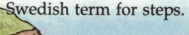

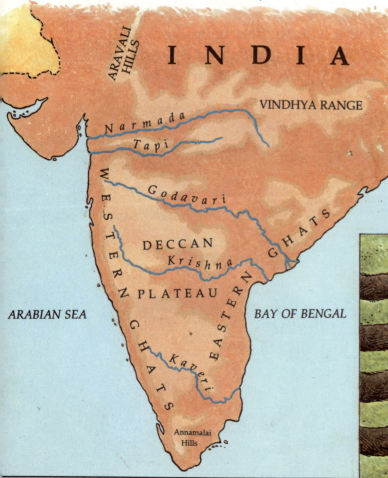

ARAVALI HILLS

I N D I A

VINDHYA RANGE

Narmada

Tapi

Godavari

WESTERN GHATS

DECCAN

Krishna

PLATEAU

EASTERN GHATS

ARABIAN SEA

BAY OF BENGAL

Kaveri

Annamalai Hills

The term *Sapta Sindhu*, collectively stands for the seven sacred rivers of India : the Ganga, Yamuna, Sindu (Indus), Godavari (Dakshin Ganga), Narmada, Krishna and Kaveri. The term occurs in prayers and in literature.

The Luni (Salt River), is the only river of Marusthali.

The Eastern and Western Ghats meet in the Nilgiri Hills in the south of India.

 Why do some rivers of the Deccan flow into the Arabian Sea while others flow into the Bay of Bengal?

The northern part of the Deccan slopes westwards, while the southern part slopes eastwards. As a result, the Narmada and the Tapi rivers flow westwards into the Arabian Sea. The Godavari, the Krishna and the Kaveri rivers, on the other hand, flow eastwards into the Bay of Bengal. Unlike the rivers of the north, which are all perennial, the peninsular rivers run dry except in the rainy season.

THAR–THE GREAT INDIAN DESERT

 How big is the Thar?

Of the 11 famous deserts in the world, the Thar is the seventh largest in area. The Sahara desert in Africa, is the largest. The Thar spreads over western India and Pakistan. It is not, however, a continuous stretch of sand but is interspersed with hillocks, salt marshes and lakes.

 Where is Marusthali?

Marusthali, meaning a dry sandy region, is an old name for that part of the Thar which lies in India. It is comprised of areas from four Indian states – Punjab, Haryana, Gujarat and Rajasthan. The Aravali range marks its eastern boundaries. In the south, it extends up to the Great Rann of Kutch. Despite efforts to halt it, the desert is spreading.

 For what is the Sambhar Lake chiefly known?

The Sambhar Lake is the saltiest lake in India. It lies nearly 60 kilometres west of Jaipur.

As the underground water in Rajasthan is salty, the lake gets encrusted with brine in summer, when the water dries up. The Sambhar yields the maximum amount of brine for salt.

The Thar desert

The Lakshadweep islands add up to a mere 32 sq.kms. They are, therefore, India's tiniest Union Territory in area as well as in population.

Kavaratti island is the headquarters of Lakshadweep. Pitti, one of the uninhabited islands, has been declared a bird sanctuary.

THE INDIAN ISLANDS

Besides the mainland, India has two groups of islands lying in the Bay of Bengal and in the Arabian Sea. They are richly diverse parts of the Indian union.

Q   Where are India's coral islands located?

Scattered in the Arabian Sea, about 300 kilometres to the west of the Kerala coast, are a group of 36 coral islands. Formerly known as Laccadive, Minicoy and Amindivi islands, they were renamed Lakshadweep (a hundred thousand islands) in 1973. Only 10 of the islands are inhabited.

Q   How many islands form the Andamans?

The Andamans are the largest group, consisting of 324 islands, of which 204 are named and only 20 are inhabited. The Andamans are separated from the Nicobar group of 22 small islands, by a deep sea named the Ten Degree Channel. The two groups of islands, however, form a single administrative unit, as a Union Territory.

Pygmalion Point (renamed Indira Point), located in the Nicobar islands, is the southern-most point of India

Corals of various shapes and colours

On April 10, 1991, India's only active volcano erupted on Barren Island in the Andamans, after lying dormant for two centuries.

Forests being the main natural wealth of the islands, the largest saw mill in the country, is located here.

 Why is the sand of Lakshadweep pure white?

Coral islands are created by tiny sea-creatures called polyps. In order to protect their soft bodies, these creatures build skeletons of calcium carbonate. When they die, these skeletons turn into large masses of white limestone. Thus, the sand found in Lakshadweep is white.

 Where are the Bay Islands?

The Bay Islands, comprising the Andaman and Nicobar islands, are strewn like beads over the blue waters of the Bay of Bengal. They form a lush green, densely forested and picturesque archipelago, which can be reached from Calcutta and Madras, by sea or by air.

 Why are the Bay Islands known as *Kala Pani*?

The colour of the water surrounding the islands looks blackish because of the incredible depth of the sea. Besides, the British used these islands as a penal settlement and built a big jail with corridors of cells radiating like the limbs of a star fish. Countless nationalists imprisoned here, had to undergo untold suffering. Today, the crumbling ruins of the old jail are the only reminders of the terrible past.

Cellular Jail at Port Blair, Andamans

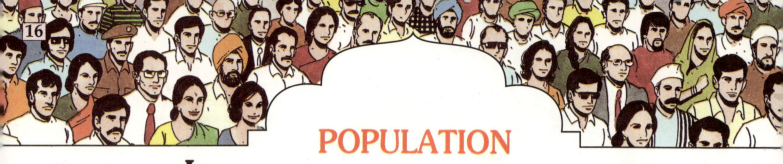

POPULATION

India is the second most populous country in the world, next only to China. India's population of over 846 million (in 1991), constituted nearly 15 per cent of the world's population of 5.66 billion (in 1994). In simple terms, every sixth person in the world is an Indian.

Q How fast is the population growing?

Despite the official population control programme launched in 1951, the population of India continues to grow indiscriminately. Each passing year witnesses an overall increase in numbers equivalent to the total population of Australia. According to the latest census data, India will be the most populous nation on earth by the year 2040.

Q Which is the most populous state of India?

According to the 1991 census, Uttar Pradesh is the most populous state in India, followed by Bihar and Maharashtra.

☐ Every minute, 50 babies are born in India.
☐ Among Indian cities, Mumbai has the largest population (12.57 million), while Calcutta ranks second with 10.86 million.

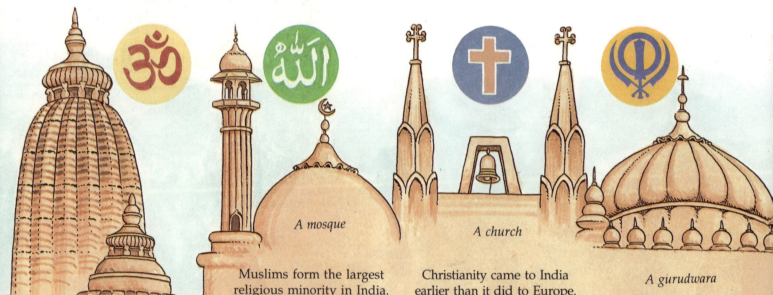

A temple

Shiva worship seems to be the most ancient living faith in India, as the discovery of a seal 4500 years old, of the Harappan culture shows.

A mosque

Muslims form the largest religious minority in India. After Indonesia and Bangladesh, India has the third largest Muslim population in the world. The Muslims, besides being divided into Sunnis and Shias, have many sub-sects such as the Khojas and the Bohras, found in Gujarat and Maharashtra.

A church

Christianity came to India earlier than it did to Europe. But it spread only during the Portuguese, Dutch, French and British occupations. Christian missionaries have made a strong impact particularly in north-eastern India. The contribution made by Christian missionaries in the field of education, has been immense.

A gurudwara

The Sikhs revere their ten Gurus and worship the holy book, *Granth Sahib*, which contains hymns composed by the Gurus and other saints of India, who were both Hindus and Muslims. The Sikh faith is marked by its openness.

RELIGIOUS COMMUNITIES

India, being a secular country, does not have a state religion. It honours all religions equally. One of the most important fundamental rights guaranteed by the Indian Constitution, is the freedom of religion and worship. Followers of all the great religions of the world are found in India.

Q **What are the major religious communities of India?**

The major religious communities are the Hindus, Muslims, Christians, Sikhs, Buddhists, Jains, Parsis and Jews.

The majority of the Indian people are Hindus. Hinduism is the oldest religion in the world, but it is hard to define. It is a way of life, a fellowship of faiths.

The Bahai faith is perhaps the only one which encompasses all religions. Its followers continue to believe in their own faith but give up ritualism, prejudice and dogmas.

A Bahai temple

A vihara

Buddhism, which was based on the Four Noble Truths of Buddha and which was adopted as the state religion by Emperor Ashoka, disappeared from the land of its origin for many centuries. At present, the neo-Buddhists who are chiefly converts, are few in number. However, Buddhism is finding a new acceptance across the world in recent years.

A derasar

The word 'Jain' is derived from Jina (the conqueror), that is, one who has conquered himself. The Jains believe that their religion was evolved by 24 *tirthankaras*, the 'perfected beings'. They believe in the sanctity of life in all forms.

An agiary

The Parsis, who worship fire, are one of the smallest communities in India and their numbers keep on dwindling with each passing year, as no conversion is allowed. However, they are also one of the most vibrant communities in India, and their contribution to all areas of professional and public life is vast and valuable.

A synagogue

The religious life of the Jews is guided by the commandments contained in the *Torah*, their sacred scripture. The oldest Indian synagogue is located in Cochin's Jew Town. A large number of Indian Jews have emigrated to Israel. India is one of the very few countries in the world, where Jews have never faced persecution.

THE PEOPLE

India is often described as an ethnic museum. This is because different races came to India at various times in history and mingled with those already there. Out of this conglomeration have evolved the diverse racial types which now inhabit India.

Q How many racial types can be discerned in India?

The people of India can be placed in six main ethnic groups. The oldest are the *adivasis* (first settlers) who came from Africa and are now found in the Andaman and Nicobar Islands.

Then there are the tribals who are largely found in the forests of central and eastern India. Another large ethnic group are the Dravidians. They inhabit the southern part of the Deccan Plateau.

The Aryans, who came from central Europe, inhabit the extensive stretch of northern India.

Later immigrants were Turks, Arabs, Persians and Afghans, all of whom contributed their racial characteristics to the Indian people. There are besides, Mongoloids akin to the tribal people of South-East Asia, who are confined to the north-eastern fringes of India. This ethnic diversity has created a rich fusion of cultures in the country.

Q Who are the Siddis?

A unique African people, the Siddis are believed to have been brought to India by Arab traders and sold to the Portuguese about 500 years ago. They live scattered along parts of the western coast of Gujarat.

Q Who are the Negroids?

The tribals of the Andamans, such as the Andamanese, Onges and Jarwas, are the surviving Negritos. Totally isolated, they lead a very primitive life. They are among the most endangered people today, numbering only a few hundred.

Q Who are the Moplahs?

The Moplahs, descendants of Arab settlers in India, are found in the northern districts of Kerala, especially Malappuram. They are the Muslims of Kerala.

 Which is the largest tribal group?

The Gonds of central India are the largest tribal group of India. The Bhils of Rajasthan rank second, while the Santhals, who are concentrated in Bihar, West Bengal and Orissa, come third.

As expert archers, the Bhils justify their name which derives from the Dravidian word for bow.

 Who were once known as the 'head-hunters' of India?

The Nagas, consisting of about 16 tribal groups, each with their own dialect, dress and customs, were once associated with warlike activities and head hunting. Many years ago, they gave up this practice and today, Nagaland is a progressive state of the Indian Union.

 How do the Meiteis differ from other inhabitants of north-eastern India?

The entire hilly region of the 'seven sisters' or the seven north-eastern states, is inhabited by people primarily of Mongoloid stock. Unlike the majority, who follow Christianity, the Meiteis of Manipur, remain as the only Vaishnavite Hindu group.

 What is the distinguishing feature of Indian society?

Caste plays a distinct role in Indian society. Its influence is primarily felt in the social activities of people. Originally, society was divided into four main groups – the Brahmins, the Kshatriyas, the Vaishyas and the Shudras – each having their separate occupations and social status. There was yet another class – the outcastes or untouchables.

In course of time, each of these groups became sub-divided into thousands of sub-castes. The expansion of education and urbanization have weakened caste prejudices. Untouchability has now been legally abolished.

 How has the diversity of its people influenced the culture of India?

India is a melting pot of many races, brought together by historical forces. This diversity has been allowed to co-exist without prejudice or persecution, ensuring the continuity of the cultural traditions of India.

There are about 5,000 languages and dialects spoken in the world.

Brahmi, spoken in Baluchistan, belongs to the Dravidian family.

LANGUAGES

Manipuri or Meithei, is one of the Tibeto-Burman languages spoken by about half a million people now.

The languages of India have evolved from different language families corresponding to the different ethnic groups that have infiltrated into India from ancient times. Thus, no Indian language can be described as 'pure', for they are all products of diverse influences.

Q How many languages are spoken in India?

India has 18 officially recognised languages. English is used as an additional official language. This is an evolution in a land where census figures have listed 1652 languages and dialects as mother tongues.

SANSKRIT HINDI
MARATHI
GUJARATI BENGALI
ASSAMESE ORIYA
NEPALI PUNJABI
MANIPURI KONKANI
KASHMIRI URDU
SINDHI

ENGLISH

TAMIL TELUGU
KANNADA
MALAYALAM

Q What are the major linguistic divisions of India?

Most Indian languages fall into two broad groups – the *Aryan* and the *Dravidian* family of languages. Most Indian languages such as Marathi, Gujarati, Bengali, Hindi and some others, belong to the Aryan family. The Dravidian languages and dialects form a distinct group by themselves and were in use much before the Aryan languages. The major Dravidian languages are Telugu, Tamil, Kannada and Malayalam.

Q Which is the oldest language of the Dravidian family?

Tamil is considered to be the oldest Dravidian language. It was spoken in some form or the other all over the Deccan as well as the Coromandel and Malabar coasts. Between the 7th and 13th centuries, these different forms of Tamil evolved into distinct languages such as Telugu, Kannada and Malayalam.

வணக்கம்

Wanakkam – greetings in Tamil

☐ Among the four Dravidian languages, Telugu is the most widely spoken in India (after Hindi, which is Aryan-derived).

The Sahitya Akademy (the National Academy of Letters) has approved 22 languages as literary languages—eleven of the Indo-Aryan family, four of the Dravidian family, plus English, Dogri, Konkani, Manipuri, Maithili, Nepali and Rajasthani.

English has taken several hundred words from Indian languages e.g. cash from the Tamil *kasu* (coin); coolie from the Kannada *kuli* and shampoo from the Hindi *champi*.

Q **What does the word 'Sanskrit' literally mean?**

The term 'Sanskrit' literally means 'perfected' or 'refined'. Sanskrit was the language of the scriptures, but, because of its strict rules of grammar and difficult pronunciation, Sanskrit became the language of the learned few. Like Latin, it is hardly spoken now-a-days, but it is listed as one of the nationally recognised languages. The Indo-Aryan languages have evolved from Sanskrit.

Q **What was Prakrit?**

As opposed to Sanskrit, Prakrit means 'natural' or 'unrefined'. It was the colloquial form of Sanskrit and was spoken by the common people. Forms of Prakrit became various dialects, varying from region to region. These regional dialects gradually evolved into the languages of the different states.

☐ Sanskrit is used in Hindu religious rituals and worship.

Namaskar – greetings in Hindi

☐ Hindi, numerically the largest of the Indo-Aryan family, is the official language of the Government of India. It is also the official language of six states. Hindi has several dialects.

Q **How did Urdu evolve?**

Urdu is the shortened name for *Zaban-e-Urdu-e-Mualla*, which means the 'language of the exalted camp or court'. The exalted camp or court refers to the military camp and court of the Muslim rulers of Delhi. The court language of the rulers was then Persian, but for communication and administration purposes, the use of a local language was necessary. Thus, a synthesis was effected and Urdu was born. Urdu developed first in the Deccan and then in Delhi. Urdu is the state language of Jammu and Kashmir.

Urdu became the literary language of famous poets such as Ibrahim Zauk and Mirza Ghalib. The noted novelist Prem Chand also wrote in Urdu.

Q **What is 'Indian English'?**

Indians have evolved their own variations of the English language, adopting many English words into the Indian languages. Known as the Hobson Jobson, Indian English, with its own colourful vocabulary and erratic grammar, has developed into an alternative, but unofficial, form of English in India.

Hindi, the official language of India, is written in the Devnagari script.

Malayalam, although a branch of the Dravidian family, developed into a distinct language with a fine script. Interestingly, the longest palindrome in the Roman script is the nine-letter word M-a-l-a-y-a-l-a-m.

SCRIPTS

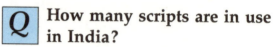

*T*he art of writing was known in India from very early times. The people of the Harappan culture used a unique pictographic script with 250 to 400 characters. Unfortunately, this script remains undeciphered, since its use 3000 years ago.

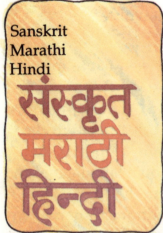

Sanskrit Marathi Hindi

Gujarati

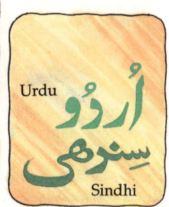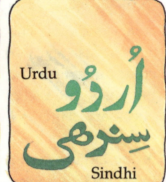

Urdu

Sindhi

Bengali

Assamese

Oriya

Punjabi (Gurmukhi)

Kannada

Telugu

Tamil

Malayalam

Q **How many scripts are in use in India?**

There are 11 major scripts used for the 18 officially recognised languages. They are Assamese, Bengali, Devnagari, Gujarati, Gurmukhi, Telugu-Kannada, Malayalam, Oriya, Persian-Arabic and Tamil. Some languages thus share a script.

Q **Which was the first deciphered Indian script?**

The Brahmi script of the Ashokan inscriptions (third century B.C.), was the first deciphered script used in India. In fact, it is the source of all Indian scripts in use today.

Q **What is Gurmukhi?**

Gurmukhi, which literally means 'from the mouth of the Guru', is the name given to the script devised by the Sikh Guru, Angad, about 400 years ago. It is commonly used for writing the Punjabi language.

☐ Brahmi, as the name suggests, was called the script of the priests (Brahmins), while Kharoshti, meaning 'ass-lip', was used by clerks. Ashoka's edicts in north-western India, were in Kharoshti.

Ashoka's edicts in Brahmi

THE POLITICAL MODEL
THE CONSTITUTION

The Constitution of India was originally in English. A Hindi translation was issued on January 24, 1950.

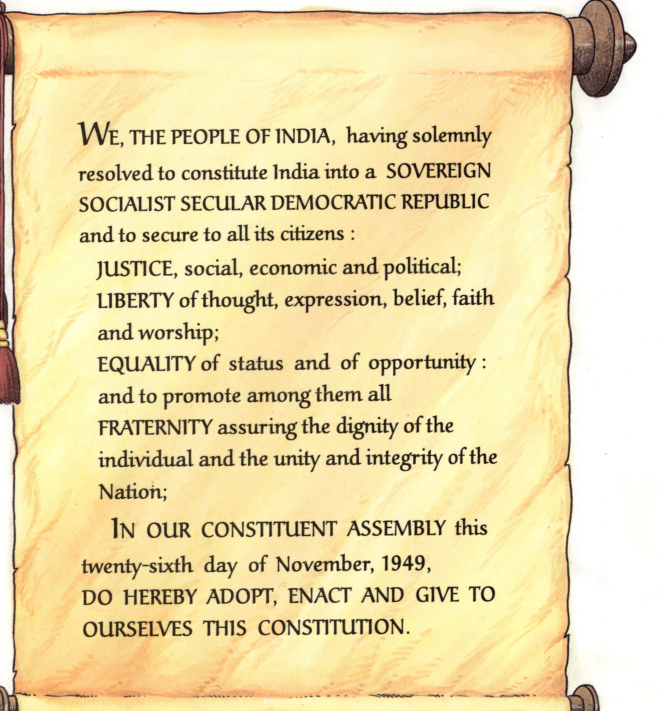

WE, THE PEOPLE OF INDIA, having solemnly resolved to constitute India into a SOVEREIGN SOCIALIST SECULAR DEMOCRATIC REPUBLIC and to secure to all its citizens :

JUSTICE, social, economic and political;
LIBERTY of thought, expression, belief, faith and worship;
EQUALITY of status and of opportunity : and to promote among them all
FRATERNITY assuring the dignity of the individual and the unity and integrity of the Nation;

IN OUR CONSTITUENT ASSEMBLY this twenty-sixth day of November, 1949, DO HEREBY ADOPT, ENACT AND GIVE TO OURSELVES THIS CONSTITUTION.

The Preamble to the Constitution.

The words, 'Socialist, secular' and 'and integrity', were added to the Preamble in 1976.

Dr. B. R. Ambedkar

The Directive Principles of State Policy lays down some objectives and enjoins the state to undertake welfare measures to achieve them. These directives are not enforceable by the judiciary.

 ## What is the Preamble?

The lines given on the previous page, form the Preamble to the Indian Constitution. It provides an introduction to the main Constitution, explaining its aims and purposes.

 ## Who prepared the Constitution?

Till 1947, the people of India did not have a Constitution. When, on August 15, India became free, the need arose for a Constitution.

The Constituent Assembly was convened and appointed a committee with Dr. B.R. Ambedkar as Chairman, to draft the Constitution. The best minds in the country worked in dedicated fashion for 2 years, 11 months and 18 days, to prepare the document.

The Constitution came into force on January 26, 1950. On that day, India declared herself to be a Sovereign Democratic Republic. Every year the day is celebrated as Republic Day.

What are the main features of the Indian Constitution?

1. The Indian Constitution is a written, comprehensive document; in fact, it is the longest constitution in the world.
2. It contains 397 articles and 12 schedules.
3. It provides for a single citizenship for the whole of India.
4. It gives the right to vote to all citizens of 18 years and above, unless they are otherwise disqualified.

5. It guarantees to all citizens certain fundamental rights.
6. It provides for an integrated, single judiciary for the whole of India.
7. Being a secular state. India honours all religions equally.

 ## Which body is the guardian of the Constitution?

The Supreme Court, consisting of the Chief Justice of India and other judges, is the guardian of the Constitution. It stands at the apex of a single integrated judicial system for the whole country. All other courts are subordinate to this body. It is the final court of appeal. It interprets the Constitution and protects the fundamental rights of citizens.

The Supreme Court, New Delhi

The Indian Constitution follows the British Parliamentary model but differs from it in one way – the Constitution is supreme and not the Parliament.

The President, besides being the Executive Head of State, is also the Supreme Commander of the Armed forces.

THE FRAMEWORK

PRESIDENT

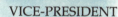

VICE-PRESIDENT

PRIME MINISTER

COUNCIL OF MINISTERS

THE PARLIAMENT

 Who is a citizen of India?

Any person who is born in India or either of whose parents was born in India or who has been a resident of India for five years immediately preceding the adoption of the Constitution, is considered to be a citizen of India.

The Constitution provides for a single citizenship for the whole of India. Every citizen is entitled to the rights and privileges enshrined in the Constitution, such as freedom of speech.

 How is the Government organised?

According to the Constitution, the Government of India is organised into the Legislature, the Executive and the Judiciary. **The Legislature** is constituted by Parliament, consisting of the two Houses; the Lok Sabha (House of the People) and the Rajya Sabha (Council of States). **The Executive** consists of the President, the Vice-President and the Council of Ministers, with the Prime Minister as the head. **The Judiciary** is represented by the Supreme Court.

 Who runs the Government?

Although the President is the Executive Head of State, it is the Prime Minister who runs the Government. He is the leader of the majority party or coalition in the Lok Sabha. He chooses the members of the Council of Ministers (Cabinet). It is the duty of the Prime Minister to communicate to the President all decisions taken by the Council of Ministers relating to the administration of the affairs of State.

Who makes laws for the country?

The Legislative (law-making) powers of the State are vested primarily in Parliament, which consists of the President and the two Houses – the Lok Sabha and the Rajya Sabha. The members of the Lok Sabha, with a strength of 545, are directly elected by the people through general elections, which are held every five years. The Rajya Sabha is a permanent body of nearly 250 members. One-third of its members retire every two years.

The Parliament House, New Delhi

Telugu-speaking people were the first to demand a separate state, Andhra, for themselves. This led to the reorganization of states along linguistic lines and with distinct boundaries.

Areawise, Madhya Pradesh is the largest state of the Union while Goa is the smallest. Maharashtra is the third largest both in terms of area and population.

Each member is thus elected for a term of 6 years. Parliament makes laws for the whole country. A bill must be passed by both Houses and approved by the President as well, before it becomes law.

 Why is India a 'Union of States'?

Shortly after independence in 1947, a demand for reorganization of states on the basis of languages spoken in the various regions, became a major issue. This resulted in the redrawing of state boundaries, as well as the establishment of new states, on the basis of language. Thus India is a Union of States and centrally-administered territories called Union Territories.

 How many states form the Indian Union?

The Union of India comprises 25 States and 7 Union Territories (1997). The Constitution provides each with a separate administrative machinery.

The organization of the State Government is similar to that of the Union Government. Each State is administered by a Governor, appointed by the President, while each Union Territory is administered by the President through an Administrator / Lieutenant Governor, also appointed by him. Like the President, the Governor is the constitutional head of the State and acts according to the advice of the Chief Minister and the Council of Ministers. State Legislatures, consisting of the Legislative Assembly (Vidhan Sabha)

and the Legislative Council (Vidhan Parishad), are empowered to formulate laws.

The State Judiciary consists of the High Court as the highest judicial body in the State, and is supported by subordinate District Courts, to dispense justice in each of its districts.

 What are the governing bodies in rural areas?

As the majority of Indians live in villages, local self-governing bodies have been formed, starting with the Gram Panchayat, at the village level and ending with the Zilla Parishad, at the district level. These are elected bodies and function for the welfare of the people.

In urban areas, local self-governing bodies have different names though their functions are similar. They are called Municipalities in cities and Corporations in metropolitan cities.

The Election Commission allots symbols to various parties and independent candidates. The symbol is important as large numbers of voters, being illiterate, identify the candidate from the symbol rather than the name.

In the 1991 general election, which was the tenth election, 520 million voters took part, making it the largest electorate in the world – it even exceeded the population of USA, which is about 320 million.

Q How is India the largest democracy in the world?

The Constitution provides for universal adult franchise, which means that all adult citizens of 18 years and above, have the right to vote for candidates of their own choice. The very first general election that took place in independent India in 1952, took four months to complete. Merely preparing lists of the names of the 173 million people who were qualified to vote, was a monumental task, especially since over 80 per cent were illiterate.

More than 17,000 candidates from 59 parties, each with a visual symbol, filed for the 3,800 seats in the state assemblies and the Lok Sabha. Nearly 200,000 polling booths had to be built, 600 million ballot papers printed, which in turn, were put into over two million ballot boxes, since each candidate then had a box of his own.

After direct elections were over, indirect elections were held to elect the President, the Vice-President, the members of the Rajya Sabha and the State Legislative Councils. Pandit Jawaharlal Nehru thus became the first Prime Minister of India and Dr. Rajendra Prasad, her first President.

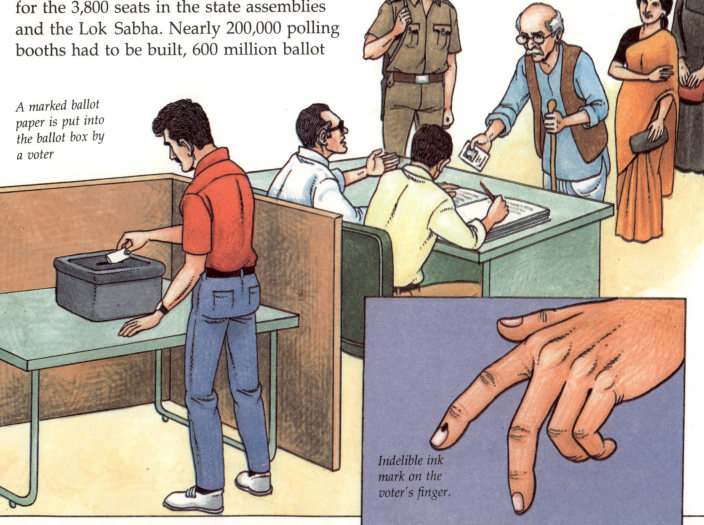

A marked ballot paper is put into the ballot box by a voter

Indelible ink mark on the voter's finger.

THE NATIONAL FLAG

The national flag, a symbol of free India, is a horizontal tricolour of saffron, white and green. The wheel in its centre, is a replica of the chakra, which appears on the abacus of Ashoka's lion capital, now at Sarnath. The flag was adopted on July 22, 1947 and presented to the nation on August 15, 1947.

Q What significance do the colours of the national flag have?

Saffron, a strong, vibrant colour, stands for courage, sacrifice and renunciation. White, symbolises truth and purity–truth in our speech and purity of thought. The freshness of green, represents life, faith and chivalry.

Q What does the wheel signify?

The 24 spokes of the wheel are multiples of 8, representing the noble precepts of the Eight-Fold Path, taught by the Buddha. The wheel itself denotes unceasing motion and progress.

Q When was the national flag first hoisted?

The national flag was hoisted for the first time on August 15, 1947, by Jawaharlal Nehru, at the historic Red Fort in Delhi. It proclaimed to the world that India was a free and independent nation. This flag replaced the British Union Jack, which had flown over India for 200 years.

Q How did the national flag evolve?

Most records indicate that the first version of the flag was unfurled at the Parsi Bagan Square (Green Park), Calcutta, in 1906.

A year later, Madame Cama and her associates, hoisted a flag of India abroad for the first time, in Germany. However, this flag was never used in India.

A third flag was designed with the Union Jack in one corner. It was, however, unacceptable to many people.

Flags of various designs were tried. Finally, a tricolour with a *charkha*, the spinning wheel, emerged. The *charkha* symbolised the people and their industry, just as it had earlier become a symbol of the national struggle for independence.

Madame Cama, 1907

1906   1917   1921   1931   1947

On July 22, 1947, three weeks before independence, the tricolour was adopted as India's national flag, replacing the *charkha* with the *chakra,* the wheel.

 Why is a flag considered necessary for a free country?

The national flag is a sacred symbol of sovereignty, as well as the ideals and aspirations of nationhood. It reminds us that we are all citizens of one nation in spite of our diversity. Every free country in the world has its own flag, symbolising the glory and collective pride of that nation. The flag stirs feelings of nationalism in its people.

 What is the Flag Code?

The flag being the symbol of a nation, is treated at all times with respect, reverence and dignity. There are rules laid down for its correct usage and display.

The flag should be hoisted at sunrise and lowered at sunset.

The flag is flown daily only from important public buildings. People may hoist it only on special days such as Independence Day (15th August), Mahatma Gandhi's birthday (2nd October), during National Week (April 6-13), observed annually in memory of the Jallianwala Bagh martyrs, Republic Day (26th January) and other days of national significance or rejoicing.

To mourn the death of a great person, Indian or foreign, the flag is flown at halfmast on government and public buildings.

The Indian team at the Olympics

The flag should not be allowed to touch the ground and may not be used as bunting, curtains and so on.

When carried in a procession, the flag should be borne high on the right shoulder of the standard bearer.

 Why was a flag *satyagraha* launched?

The tricolour with the *charkha* became popular as a symbol of freedom. Thousands of full-sized and miniature flags were made and distributed all over the country. Alarmed, the British government prohibited its use. So a flag *satyagraha* was launched in 1923, at Nagpur. Thousands took out processions carrying the flag. The British were compelled to lift orders banning the flag during processions.

The words, *Satyameva Jayate*, form the opening phrase of a verse of the *Mundaka Upanishad*

THE NATIONAL EMBLEM

The national emblem is an adaptation of the capital (upper portion) of Ashoka's pillar, now at Sarnath. The emblem, however, shows only three of the four lions which are visible on the Ashokan pillar. The wheel portrayed in the centre of the abacus, has a bull to the right and a horse to the left. The pillar, however, also has an elephant and a rhinoceros at the back. The words Satyameva Jayate, meaning 'Truth alone triumphs', are inscribed below the abacus in the Devnagari script.

Q Why is an emblem necessary?

Every free nation has a national emblem. It appears prominently on things connected with the Government. The emblem represents the authority of the nation. It is used exclusively for official purposes.

Q Where do we see the national emblem used?

The emblem is used on all official stationery and seals of the Government of India. It also appears on Government publications and films produced by the Films Division. Coins, currency notes all carry the emblem prominently. Indian missions abroad use the emblem on their crockery and cutlery.

The national emblem on currency and postage

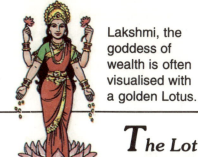

Lakshmi, the goddess of wealth is often visualised with a golden Lotus.

THE NATIONAL FLOWER

Traditionally, Indian poets have used the Lotus to represent female beauty. The eyes are compared with Lotus buds, the hands with full-blown flowers and the arms with the flower's graceful roots.

*T*he Lotus, a symbol of beauty, purity and integrity, is the national flower of India. Rising as it does, from the muddy bottoms of lakes and ponds, the lotus reveals its beauty in a unique way.

Q How is the Lotus formed?

The Lotus has fragrant flowers, usually white or pink. The stems are hollow and straight while the leaves are waterproof because of a network of small, closely-set hairs. After the Lotus has bloomed, the seeds, each in its separate compartment, are housed in a flat-topped pod that resembles a shower-head.

Q When does the Lotus bloom?

The Lotus loves sunshine and warmth and flowers mainly in summer and after the rains. This highly extolled plant is, however, also edible. Its roots are cooked while the seeds are used in Ayurvedic medicine.

Q Why is the Lotus a symbol of a wise man?

The Lotus usually grows in muddy waters but remains untouched by the dirt and mire from which it emerges. In the same way, a wise man remains unaffected by worldly attachments and leads a life of righteousness.

Q How is the Lotus associated with Lord Buddha?

According to legend, when Prince Siddhartha was to be born, the queen dreamt that a spotless, white elephant with a white Lotus in its trunk, entered her womb.

Another legend states that when Siddhartha was born, he took seven steps and Lotus flowers sprang from each footprint. Thus a Lotus came to symbolise his birth.

The Buddha is usually shown seated on an open Lotus in the *yogic* Lotus position.

Lord Brahma, the creator of the world, is shown seated on a Lotus which emerged from the navel of Lord Vishnu, the Preserver.

Lord Buddha

THE NATIONAL ANTHEM

Rabindranath Tagore was awarded the prestigious Nobel Prize for literature, for his *Gitanjali*. He was the first Asian to receive this honour.

Jana-gana-mana, an inspiring song composed by the great poet, Rabindranath Tagore, is the national anthem of India. The complete song consists of five stanzas, but only the first stanza constitutes the full version of the national anthem. It is sung on all occasions of national importance.

 What is the playing time of the national anthem?

The playing time of the full version of the anthem is about 52 seconds. Under no circumstances should it be played for more than a minute. On certain occasions, the shorter version consisting of the first and last lines of the stanza (playing time about 20 seconds), is played. Whenever the national anthem is played, people are required to stand as a mark of respect.

 What was the original title of the song?

The song, in Bengali, was first published under the title *Bharat Vidhata*, in a magazine (*Tattvabodhini Patrika*), of which Rabindranath Tagore was the editor. The poet himself translated it into English under the title, *The Morning Song of India.*

THE MORNING SONG OF INDIA
(English translation of the national anthem)

Thou art the ruler of the minds of all people, dispenser of India's destiny. Thy name rouses the hearts of the Punjab, Sind, Gujarat and Maratha, of the Dravid and Orissa and Bengal; it echoes in the hills of the Vindhyas and Himalayas, mingles in the music of the Jamuna and Ganges and is chanted by the waves of the Indian Sea. They pray for thy blessings and sing thy praise. The saving of all people waits in thy hand, thou, dispenser of India's destiny. Victory, victory, victory to thee.

 How did the song become the national anthem?

Soon after independence, on August 15, 1947, it became obvious that *God Save the King* was unsuitable for a free country. India needed her own anthem. Matters came to a head when in 1947, the Indian delegation to the United Nations was asked for its national anthem, which was to be played on a particular occasion. As no official anthem existed at the time, a record of *Jana-gana-mana* was handed over. Accordingly, the song was picked up and played by the UN orchestra. As it was greatly acclaimed by all, *Jana-gana-mana* was adopted as the national anthem on January 24, 1950.

 When is the national anthem played?

The national anthem is played on Republic Day and Independence Day, (January 26 and August 15), every year, at the time of the unfurling of the national flag.

It is also played at the national salute given to the President of the Republic of India, Governors of States and visiting foreign heads, as well as on all ceremonial occasions in fields as diverse as sports, culture and education.

Bankim Chandra Chatterji (1830–1895), was a Bengali poet and novelist. Besides *Anand Math*, his other famous novels are, *Durgeshnandini* and *Kapal Kundala*.

THE NATIONAL SONG

Vande Mataram is the national song of India. It was composed by Bankim Chandra Chatterji, set to music by Rabindranath Tagore and translated into English by Aurobindo Ghosh – thus bringing together three of the greatest minds India has produced.

VANDE MATARAM

Vandé Mātaram!
Sujalām, suphalām, malayaja, shitalām!
Shasyashyāmalam, Mātaram!
Shubhrajyotsnā pulakitayāminim,
Phullakusumita drumadala shobhinim,
Suhāsinim, sumadhura bhāshinim,
Sukhadām, varadām, Mātaram!

VANDE MATARAM

(English translation by Sri Aurobindo)

I bow to thee, Mother
richly-watered, richly-fruited
cool with the winds of the south
dark with the crops of the harvests,

The Mother!

Her nights rejoicing in the glory of the
    moonlight
her lands clothed beautifully with her trees
    in flowering bloom
sweet of laughter, sweet of speech

The Mother, giver of boons, giver of bliss

 When was the song first sung?

The song, *Vande Mataram*, occurs in Bankim Chandra's Bengali novel, *Ananda Math* and was first sung at a political meeting in 1896. The song gained immediate and lasting recognition as a hymn to India and a call for unity and strength.

 Why was *Vande Mataram* not adopted as the national anthem?

Vande Mataram, enjoys much the same status as that of *Jana-Gana-Mana*. However, it did not become the national anthem due to the fact that it did not lend itself to harmonization, according to experts.

In an era of national awareness, several songs vied for national recognition. Among these, the song Sare Jahan Se Achchha Hindustan Hamara, *written by Sir Mohammed Iqbal (1876–1939), became immensely popular and is sung with great feeling even today.*

Q **What is the meaning of *Vande Mataram*?**

The words *Vande Mataram* mean 'Hail Motherland'. *Vande* translates as 'I bow' and *Mataram* as 'mother' or 'motherland'. These two words of the song became the powerful battle cry of the Indians in their struggle for freedom.

The Indian Posts and Telegraph Department issued a stamp on January 24, 1976, to commemorate Jim Corbett's birth centenary.

THE NATIONAL ANIMAL

The majestic tiger, the largest member of the cat family, is the national animal of India. It is a symbol of power and speed. In fact, the name 'tiger' derives from the Greek word for arrow. Nearly two-thirds of the world's tiger population is found in India. Free tigers are found only in Asia. It was in 1972, that the tiger was chosen as the national animal. Earlier, this honour was enjoyed by the lion.

Q What is 'Project Tiger'?

Tiger-shooting was once considered a great sport by Indian royals. Important visitors to India were also encouraged to shoot tigers. Others hunted tigers for their valuable skins and bones. As a result of indiscriminate killing, the tiger population started decreasing and shrank from 40,000 to 1,814 in just 50 years. So, to protect them, a national scheme called Project Tiger, was launched with the help of the World Wildlife Fund. Certain areas were declared 'tiger reserves', where tigers could live safely in their natural habitat, protected from human greed and insensitivity.

Q How is a Tiger Census carried out in India?

Counting tigers is not as easy as counting humans. Fortunately, every tiger has distinctive pugmarks, just as every human has distinctive finger prints. So the people who carry out the census, carefully count the number of different pugmarks around waterholes in various forests. By computing the number of pugmarks, we know the number of tigers in the country.

Q How are the tigers at the Sundarbans National Park (West Bengal) unique?

In the mangrove forests of the Sundarbans, the Indian tiger is popularly called the Royal Bengal Tiger. Unlike in other habitats, the tiger here lives both on land and in water and spends long periods of time in saline water. The Sundarbans form the largest tiger sanctuary in the world.

A Royal Bengal Tiger

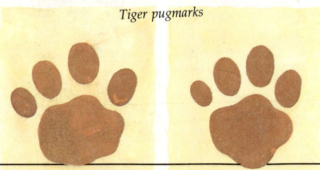

Tiger pugmarks

It is believed that at least one tiger is killed every day for its bones and skin. Tiger bones are used in medicine while its skin is prized as a decorative item.

Q **Are there white tigers?**

For many years there were intriguing reports about the existence of white tigers in India. Then in 1951, a shooting party in the forests of Rewa, in Madhya Pradesh, captured a litter of 4 cubs, one of which was white. This white male cub grew into a large, white tiger, mated and fathered many other white tigers. Today, all the white tigers found in India and abroad are descendants of the single white cub found in 1951. Nandankanan, in Orissa, is the world's first White Tiger Safari.

A white tiger

Q **Why does a tiger become a man-eater?**

Tigers, as a rule, do not prey on humans. They attack human beings only if wounded or too old to hunt wild animals. But once a tiger has tasted human blood, it becomes a dangerous man-eater. In areas close to forests where tigers are found, people live under the constant fear of tiger-attack.

Q **Who was Jim Corbett? Why is a national park named after him?**

Edward James Corbett or Jim Corbett, as he is popularly known, was a great lover of wildlife. However, when tigers became man-eaters in the Garhwal region, he undertook the dangerous task of tracking and shooting them. It is said that Corbett shot 12 man-eaters that had killed over 1,500 people. Through his efforts, a game sanctuary known as Hailey National Park, was established in 1936, in Uttar Pradesh. This park was later renamed Corbett National Park, in recognition of his services and was the first sanctuary to come under the 'Project Tiger' scheme.

Jim Corbett

36

Lord Krishna gave the peacock dignity and glory by wearing its feather in his crown.

THE NATIONAL BIRD

The peacock is the mount of Kartikeya, also called Skanda, the god of war.

The magnificent peacock is the national bird of India. Known as mor *in Hindi and* mayura *and* nilkantha, *in Sanskrit, the peacock has always enjoyed a unique status and dignity in India.*

Q **Why is the peacock called the 'thousand-eyed creature' in Sanskrit?**

The peacock is perhaps the most beautiful among male birds, with its long blue neck, fan-shaped crest, and its gorgeous train or tail of feathers. Each feather ends in a half-moon or 'eye'. When raised, the tail spreads like a fan from which a thousand eyes seem to gaze. Ironically, the female or peahen, is a small, drab bird in comparison, without the sweeping train.

Q **Why does the peacock dance?**

The peacock, although a shy bird, dances in front of the peahens during courtship. He then struts before them showing off his many-coloured train.

☐ Alexander the Great was so fascinated with the peacock, that he took back to Greece several peacocks from India.

☐ The throne of the Mughal Emperor Shahjahan, was called the Peacock Throne because it had gem-studded peacocks on it. This fabled treasure was taken to Iran by the invader Nadir Shah.

☐ Peacocks shed their tail feathers once a year and grow new ones. People carefully collect these old feathers, which are then made into lovely fans and other decorative items.

Sometimes, Saraswati, the goddess of learning, is shown with the peacock.

Decorative peacock feather fans

The sight of rain clouds is another occasion for such display, perhaps to hail the arrival of rain after the long hot summer. The peacock's lordly strutting has also given rise to the commonly used phrases, 'proud as a peacock' and 'as vain as a peacock'.

Q Where are white peacocks found?

The white peacock is a rare variety. It is found only in the forests of Assam. Some zoos also have them.

A white peacock

Q Which Indian emperor forbade the killing of peacocks?

The bloody battle of Kalinga in 260 BC, moved Emperor Ashoka to embrace Buddhism. *Ahimsa* or non-violence, became an important principle of his life. He completely forbade the killing of peacocks which were slaughtered daily for the royal kitchen.

In Gujarat and Rajasthan, peacocks are regarded as sacred and inviolate. Flocks of them can be seen entering villages looking for grain and shoots.

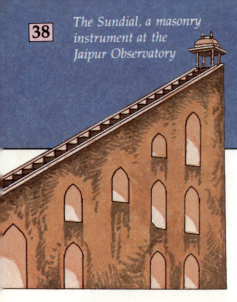

The Sundial, a masonry instrument at the Jaipur Observatory

THE NATIONAL CALENDAR

*T*he national calendar of India, based on the Saka Era, has a normal year of 365 days, with the new year falling on Chaitra 1 (March 22). The names of the months are– Chaitra, Vaishakh, Jyeshtha, Ashadh, Shravan, Bhadrapad, Ashwin, Kartik, Margashirsha, Poush, Magh and Phalgun.

 How does the national calendar correspond with the Gregorian calendar?

The Gregorian calendar is used by nations all over the world. Therefore, in order to synchronise the national calendar with the dates of the International calendar, it was decided that *Chaitra 1* would always fall on March 22, in a normal year and on March 21, in a leap year.

 How many years is the national calendar behind the Gregorian calendar?

The national calendar came into force on March 22, 1957. Its corresponding date was *Chaitra 1*, 1879 Saka. Hence, the national calendar is 78 years behind the Gregorian calendar.

 What is the Saka Era?

From ancient times, attempts have been made to measure and record time in many different ways. There are various eras and calendars used in the country. The Saka Era is one of them. It was instituted by a Saka Kushan king, perhaps Kanishka. He introduced the era in 78 AD to mark his power and glory.

King Kanishka

 What is a lunar month?

The lunar month is the duration in which the moon makes one complete revolution around the earth. It is calculated from one new moon to the next and has a span of $29\frac{1}{2}$ days. Thus, 12 lunar months make only 354 days.

Consequently, the lunar year falls short of the solar year by about 11 days. The Muslims, who follow a purely lunar reckoning, thus have their Ramzan fast falling in different months of the International calendar.

 What is the Hindu calendar?

A majority of Indians follow the traditional Hindu calendar based on a luni-solar reckoning for the celebration of festivals, marriages and other auspicious occasions. The shortfall of 11 days

A page from a panchang *(almanac)*

between the lunar and solar years is adjusted over a period of 3 years, when an additional month, *adhik-mas* (extra month), is added on. Indians are probably the first people to evolve and use a luni-solar calendar.

 What is the *Panchang* (Almanac)?

The *Panchang* (five limbs) is a book of tables, containing a calendar of months and days with astronomical data and calculations, days of festivals and *muhurtams* (auspicious times), besides other useful information.

Every year, astronomers from all over India meet at the Jaipur Observatory and prepare the almanac with the help of various instruments built more than 250 years ago by Sawai Raja Jai Singh.

A majority of Indians still consult the traditional Hindu calendar and almanac. But, as the almanac is complicated, the common man depends upon priests to interpret it and so fix the *muhurta* for special events such as festivals, marriages and other auspicious occasions.

 What is Indian Standard Time?

In olden days, people calculated time by the position of the sun with the help of sundials. But, since the earth rotates around itself once every 24 hours, different places on the earth face the sun at different times. As a result, time changes from place to place. Hence, there existed a difference of about 30° longitude, or 2 hours, in terms of local time between the eastern-most and the western-most

parts of India. Therefore, the local time of a place situated midway between these two extremes, near Allahabad, with a longitude of $82\frac{1}{2}°$, was adopted as the standard time for the whole of India. This official time is used by the Indian Railways, post offices, Akashvani (All India Radio) and others.

Q **How far ahead of Greenwich Mean Time is Indian Standard Time (IST)?**

Indian Standard Time is $5\frac{1}{2}$ hours ahead of Greenwich Mean Time (GMT).

Greenwich is a borough of London, England. The time there is used as the basis for calculating time in most of the world. For this, a system of time zones has been introduced. There are 24 zones, one for each hour of the day and night. The 12 zones that are to the east, are ahead of Greenwich time, and the 12 zones that are to the west, are behind Greenwich time.

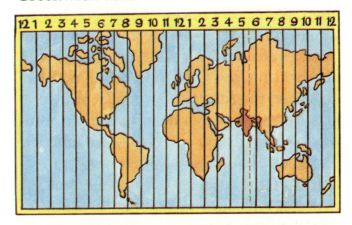

The Standard Time of Pakistan, is half an hour behind IST, while that of Bangladesh is half an hour ahead of IST.

Pakistan	India	Bangladesh
5.30 p.m.	6.00 p.m.	6.30 p.m.

NATIONAL DAYS

REPUBLIC DAY

Republic Day is India's greatest national celebration, observed throughout the country on January 26 every year. In the capital, New Delhi, the festivities are the most spectacular, and the day is celebrated with parade and pageantry. Watched by a vast multitude of people, the parade starts from Rashtrapati Bhavan (the presidential residence) and winding its way through the heart of the city, ends at the historic Red Fort in Old Delhi.

Q **What is the significance of January 26?**

January 26 is a special day for India as on this day, in 1950, the country became a sovereign democratic republic with a written constitution and elected parliament. The day imparts a feeling of pride and confidence to the people.

Q **How did a country of Rajas and Maharajas become a democratic republic?**

At the time of independence, although India was under British rule, there were 565 Princely States, big and small, ruled by powerful sovereigns who were protected by treaties of alliance with the British Crown. Without bringing them together, the fundamental unity of the country was not possible. This unification was accomplished by Sardar Vallabhbhai Patel, whose statesmanship helped to integrate the country into one nation, without bitterness or fighting. In a little less than two years, all the Princely States became a part of the Republic of India.

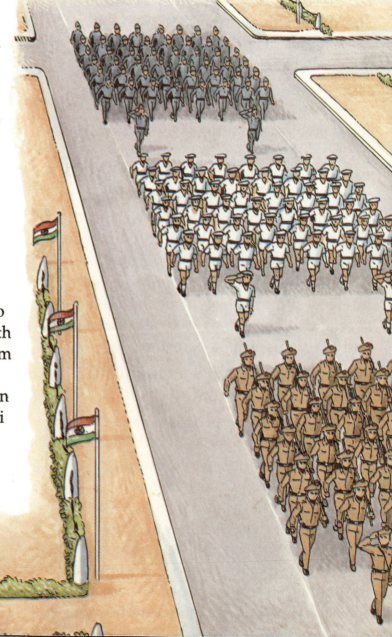

Q **Where was the first Republic Day parade held?**

The first Republic Day parade in 1950, was held at the Irwin Stadium (the present day National Stadium). The press handout read, 'The President, who will take the oath of office in the morning, will drive in State at 2:30 in the afternoon to Irwin Stadium... The hoisting of the national flag by the President, and a parade of units representing all the armed forces will be the highlights of the ceremonies...'

Since 1952, the parade is held in the morning instead of in the afternoon, nor is it confined to the stadium.

Q **Why is a Republic Day parade held?**

It was the British who brought to India the concept of the ceremonial parade. It was used for both celebration and national glorification. The Republic Day parade, once a small and modest affair, has now turned into a lavish spectacle of marching columns representing the armed forces, accompanied by armoured vehicles and military bands. These are followed by decorated floats presented by the various states of India and folk dancers drawn from the diverse regions of the country. An air display by the Indian Air Force, forms the highlight of the parade.

Q **How do the Republic Day celebrations end?**

Three days later, on the evening of January 29, a stirring ceremony known as 'Beating Retreat', is held. The ancient military custom of sending drummers through the streets just before sunset to warn the troops to return to their barracks before the colours were hauled down for the night, has been revived in a unique way. Twenty or more bands, from the three services, perform. But it does not end there. The plaintive notes of the old hymn, *Abide With Me* (also a favourite of Mahatma Gandhi), are played. The bands then fall silent although the hymn has not concluded. In the poignant silence, a solitary bugler takes up the hymn's refrain. The final notes fade away – marking the end of the Republic Day celebrations.

Not far from the famous Golden Temple in Amritsar, there is a well-maintained garden. Here stands a huge pylon, built in honour of those who died at Jallianwala Bagh.

Rabindranath Tagore renounced the knighthood conferred on him by the British Government, in protest against the massacre at Jallianwala Bagh.

NATIONAL WEEK

more wounded. The General left without offering any medical assistance to the wounded and dying.

The news of the massacre was first suppressed by the British authorities, but when it broke, the whole country was stunned and horrified.

Q **How did the British Government react to the Jallianwala massacre?**

Public outcry in India compelled the British Government to enquire into the events leading to the massacre at the Jallianwala Bagh. Although General Dyer was asked to resign, he was proclaimed a hero by the House of Lords, for his 'valiant services' to the Crown. Funds were raised on his behalf and he was presented with a bejewelled sword on which was inscribed, *Saviour of the Punjab*!

General Dyer

Q **Why is National Week observed?**

Every year, from April 6 to 13, National Week is observed in memory of the people who were massacred at Jallianwala Bagh, in Amritsar, on April 13, 1919.

It was the day of the Baisakhi festival. Thousands of men, women and children had gathered at Jallianwala Bagh to hear their leaders. While the meeting was in progress, General Dyer arrived with troops. With no prior warning and without any provocation, he ordered the troops to open fire. There was no way of escape as the only exit was blocked by the army. The firing stopped only when the ammunition had run out. Over 1000 innocent people were killed and many

Q **What precipitated the Jallianwala massacre?**

In March 1919, the British Government passed the Rowlatt Act. It allowed the British Government to arrest any person merely on suspicion and detain him without trial, with no right of appeal. Gandhiji and other leaders protested against the Act, calling it the 'Black Act'. It was at one of these protest meetings that the massacre took place. The tragedy changed the course of Indian history and paved the way for an independent India.

Two other countries—South Korea and Bahrain—celebrate their countries' independence days on August 15, too.

In 1947, 15th August happened to fall on a Friday. As soon as the radio announced the date, astrologers all over India began to consult their charts and proclaimed the day to be so inauspicious that India 'would be better advised to tolerate the British one day longer rather than risk eternal damnation'!

INDEPENDENCE DAY

India celebrates August 15, as Independence Day every year. It is the most significant of our national days because on this day in 1947, India became a free country after nearly two centuries of British overlordship. It is thus a day of dedication for her people, as well as one of celebration. At the historic Red Fort in Delhi, the Prime Minister of India hoists the national flag and addresses the nation.

Q When were the following words spoken?

"Long years ago, we made a tryst with destiny and now the time comes when we shall redeem our pledge..."

On the night bridging the 14th and 15th August, 1947, Jawaharlal Nehru spoke these immortal words in the Constituent Assembly, which is today called the Parliament.

Thousands of people had gathered outside the Assembly building to celebrate the transfer of power. As midnight struck, bells chimed and conch shells blew, there was great joy and rejoicing throughout the whole country.

In the morning, Jawaharlal Nehru as the first Prime Minister of India, unfurled the national flag on the ramparts of the Red Fort. It was the symbolic pledge of a new nation as well as a tribute to all those who had fought for Indian independence.

Q Why was the Red Fort at Delhi selected for the independence ceremony?

The Red Fort, built by the great Mughal Emperor Shah Jahan, was the seat of Bahadur Shah Zafar, the last Mughal Emperor, when he was declared the Emperor of Hindustan during the 1857 uprising against the British. Thus, Netaji Subhash Bose, head of the exiled Azad Hind Government, wished to hoist the flag of free India from the Red Fort.

It was therefore, in a symbolic meeting of past and present on the ramparts of the Red Fort, that on 15th August, 1947, India ushered in a new dawn and the promise of a new beginning.

The Red Fort, Delhi

It was the poet Rabindranath Tagore, who first called Gandhi the 'Mahatma' or a 'Great Soul'.

To commemorate the Gandhi Centenary in 1969, no less than 41 countries issued Gandhi stamps. Of these, the British stamp is considered outstanding.

GANDHI JAYANTI

The birth anniversary of Mahatma Gandhi is celebrated with reverence on October 2, every year, all over India. Homage is paid to the great leader by holding prayer meetings and by spinning charkhas. In Delhi, people gather at his samadhi at Rajghat, to offer floral tributes. Verses from the various scriptures are recited, and his favourite hymn is sung – Raghu Pati Raghava Raja Ram, Patit Pavan Sita Ram.

Gandhi was the 'Father of the Nation' (Bapu), a great soul (Mahatma) and the gentle prophet of a non-violent revolution, all rolled into one. He criss-crossed his country on foot and in third-class railway carriages to stress his identity with the impoverished masses. He had tea at Buckingham Palace with the King-Emperor, dressed in the homespun cotton chaddar and loincloth that were his trademarks. He practised a life of spartan simplicity. The symbol of his challenge to the age of imperialism was the primitive wooden spinning wheel on which he laboured religiously every day. Amidst all the violence, hatred and pettiness rife in modern society, he was a person who believed in the dignity of man and left us all a legacy of ahimsa, love and tolerance.

Lead me from the Unreal to the Real, From Darkness to light, From Death to Immortality.

> –The Vedic verse chanted at Gandhiji's funeral pyre.

I would like to see India free and strong so that she may offer herself as a willing and pure sacrifice for the betterment of the world....
I want Khudai Raj, the kingdom of God on earth.

–Mahatma Gandhi

Words inscribed in Hindi and English on a plaque beside his *samadhi* at Raj Ghat.

Mahatma Gandhi's samadhi

The Government of India wished to honour Gandhiji on his 80th birthday (2 Oct. 1948), by issuing a set of Gandhi stamps.

Following his assassination, these were issued as 'mourning stamps' on 15th Aug. 1948, the first anniversary of independence. Among them was a unique trilingual stamp in English, Hindi and Urdu.

Gandhi was the great apostle of Peace.
— The Dalai Lama

Some of the tributes paid to Mahatma Gandhi by national and international personalities, soon after his assassination in 1948…

The light has gone out of our lives and there is darkness everywhere. Our beloved leader, Bapu, as we called him, the Father of the Nation, is no more… And yet I am wrong, for the light that shone in this country was no ordinary light… a thousand years later, that light will still be seen…

— Pandit Jawaharlal Nehru
Addressing the nation on Gandhiji's assassination.

Generations to come… will scarcely believe that such a one as this (Gandhi) ever in flesh and blood walked upon this earth.

— Albert Einstein

Gandhiji is an apostle of ahimsa, *a founder of a new religion and everything pales into insignificance in his view before* ahimsa.

— Bipin Chandra Pal

Gandhi never claimed to be any other than an ordinary man. He admitted that he had frequently learnt by his mistakes. He was the universal brother, lover and friend of poor, weak, suffering humanity. Let us all do homage to his spirit, not by words alone but by dedicating our lives as he did to the pursuit of truth, the love of our fellowmen, the healing of wounds of nations.

— Lord Pethick-Lawrence

We cannot all be Gandhis, but we could in a lesser or greater degree imbibe the essence of his teachings, the deeper truths for which he lived and died.

— G.L. Mehta

Dr. Martin Luther King (1929–1968), a black American clergyman, was greatly influenced by Gandhiji's philosophy of *satyagraha* (non-violent struggle). He adopted the same strategy of civil disobedience in the black struggle for equality. Like Gandhiji, he too, was assassinated – in 1968, in Memphis, Tennessee.

Dr. Martin Luther King

Rabindranath Tagore : was awarded the Nobel Prize for Literature in 1913.

C. V. Raman : was awarded the Nobel Prize for Physics, in 1930.

Hargobind Khorana : now an American citizen, was awarded the Nobel Prize for Medicine, in 1968.

NATIONAL AWARDS

*T*he Government of India has instituted a system of awards as tokens of recognition for distinguished service, exceptional performance or outstanding contribution, in the spheres of social service, the arts, the sciences and literature. They are also conferred for acts of gallantry, both on and off the battle-field, as well as in other service areas. These awards fall into four categories–civilian awards, gallantry awards, distinguished service awards and sports awards.

Q How does the Param Vir Chakra award differ from the Ashoka Chakra award?

Both these awards are gallantry awards, conferred for valour and bravery.

The Param Vir Chakra, the highest decoration, is awarded for conspicuous bravery or some courageous act of daring or self-sacrifice in the presence of the enemy, on land, at sea or in the air.

The Mahavir Chakra and the Vir Chakra, are the second and third awards in this category. All three awards are given to members of the Armed Forces.

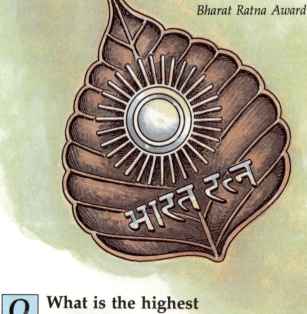

Bharat Ratna Award

Q What is the highest civilian award?

Bharat Ratna, the highest of civilian awards, is given in recognition of public service of the most outstanding order, or for distinguished work in the fields of art, science or literature. The other civilian awards conferred are, Padma Vibhushan, Padma Bhushan and Padma Shri, in that order of precedence.

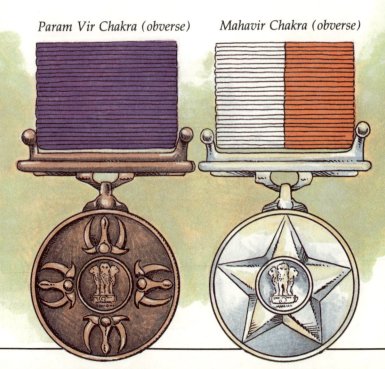

Param Vir Chakra (obverse) *Mahavir Chakra (obverse)*

Mother Teresa : was awarded the Nobel Prize for Peace, in 1979.

Subramanian Chandrasekhar : an American citizen of Indian origin, was awarded the Nobel Prize for Physics, in 1983. [he was a nephew of C. V. Raman].

Dalai Lama : spiritual leader of the Tibetans, living in India since 1959, was awarded the Nobel Prize for Peace, in 1989.

The Ashoka Chakra is awarded for acts of gallantry other than in the face of the enemy, such as in maintaining law and order or for conspicuous gallantry in civilian service. The other awards in this category are the Kirti Chakra and the Shaurya Chakra. Both civilians and servicemen are eligible for these decorations.

Arjuna Award

Ashoka Chakra (obverse)

All of these awards may be conferred posthumously.

 What is the Arjuna Award?

The Arjuna Award, named after Arjuna, the great hero of the epic *Mahabharata,* is given annually to outstanding sportspersons. The award was instituted in 1961, with a view to extending encouragement and recognition to sporting achievements in various disciplines. It carries a cash prize of Rs. 50,000, a bronze statue of the epic hero Arjuna, a scroll and a personal kit.

 Who gets the Dronacharya Award?

This award is given to outstanding sports coaches in recognition of their dedicated services in training sportspersons to levels of excellence. The award, named after Guru Dronacharya, who taught archery and other sports to the Kaurava and Pandava princes of the *Mahabharata,* was instituted in 1985. The award comprises a plaque, a scroll, a blazer, a tie and a cash prize of Rs. 75,000.

 When are the national awards announced?

The awards are announced once a year on Republic Day (January 26). They were, however, announced for the first time, on August 15, 1954.

As a special gesture of honour, the President decorated the first Prime Minister of India, Jawaharlal Nehru, with the award of Bharat Ratna, on July 15, 1955, in recognition of his outstanding services to the nation.

48

The Bharat Award, another national bravery award for children, was given to Prahlad Singh of village Mundawa, U.P., who saved the lives of his five schoolmates when they were all attacked by a large black bear. In this incident, Prahlad lost one eye and a portion of his jaw. He received the award in 1995.

 Who are the recipients of the Geeta and Sanjay Chopra Awards?

These awards are conferred on those children who have performed outstanding deeds of bravery. Each awardee receives a silver medal, a certificate and a cash prize.

The awards, instituted in 1978, are named after Geeta Chopra and her brother Sanjay Chopra. Both children died struggling to free themselves from two criminals. In order to encourage other children to follow their example of brave conduct and to give due recognition to courageous children, the awards were instituted and are declared on November 14, Children's Day, every year. The recipients also take an honoured part in the Republic Day parade, riding on caparisoned elephants.